Baby Goats

2022
12 MONTH CALENDAR

Please use Binder clip or push pin to hang
so you can preserve the photos for later use.

Thank you for your purchase!

January

Sunday	Monday	Tuesday	Wednesday	Thursday	Friday	Saturday
						1 New Year's Day
2 New Moon ●	3	4	5	6	7	8
9 First Quarter ◗	10	11	12	13	14	15
16	17 Martin Luther King Jr. Day Full Wolf Moon ○	18	19	20	21	22
23 / 30	24 / 31	25 Last Quarter ◗	26	27	28	29

February

Sunday	Monday	Tuesday	Wednesday	Thursday	Friday	Saturday
		1 **First Day of Black History Month** New Moon ●	2 **Groundhog Day**	3	4	5
6	7	8 First Quarter ◐	9	10	11	12
13	14 **Valentine's Day**	15	16 Full Snow Moon ○	17	18	19
20	21 **Presidents' Day (Regional Holiday)**	22	23 Last Quarter ◐	24	25	26
27	28					

March

Sunday	Monday	Tuesday	Wednesday	Thursday	Friday	Saturday
		1	2 First Day of Women's History Month New Moon ●	3	4	5
6	7	8	9	10 First Quarter ◐	11	12
13	14	15	16	17 St. Patrick's Day	18 Full Worm Moon ○	19
20 Spring Equinox	21	22	23	24	25 Last Quarter ◑	26
27	28	29	30	31		

April

Sunday	Monday	Tuesday	Wednesday	Thursday	Friday	Saturday
					1 New Moon ●	2
3	4	5	6	7	8	9 First Quarter ◗
10	11	12	13	14	15	16 Full Pink Moon ○
17 Easter Sunday	18 Tax Day	19	20	21	22 Earth Day	23 Last Quarter ◗
24	25	26	27	28	29	30 New Moon ●

May

Sunday	Monday	Tuesday	Wednesday	Thursday	Friday	Saturday
1	2	3	4	5 Cinco de Mayo	6	7
8 Mother's Day	9 First Quarter ◐	10	11	12	13	14
15	16 Full Flower Moon **Eclipse** ○	17	18	19	20	21
22 Last Quarter ◑	23	24	25	26	27	28
29	30 Memorial Day New Moon ●	31				

June

Sunday	Monday	Tuesday	Wednesday	Thursday	Friday	Saturday
			1	2	3	4
5	6	7 First Quarter ◑	8	9	10	11
12	13	14 Full Strawberry Moon ○	15	16	17	18
19 Father's Day Juneteenth	20	21 Summer Solstice Last Quarter ◐	22	23	24	25
26	27	28	29 New Moon ●	30		

July

Sunday	Monday	Tuesday	Wednesday	Thursday	Friday	Saturday
					1	2
3	4 Independence Day	5	6	7 First Quarter ◑	8	9
10	11	12	13 Full Buck Moon ○	14	15	16
17	18	19	20	21 Last Quarter ◐	22	23
24 / 31	25	26	27	28 New Moon ●	29	30

August

Sunday	Monday	Tuesday	Wednesday	Thursday	Friday	Saturday
	1	2	3	4	5 First Quarter ◑	6
7	8	9	10	11	12 Full Sturgeon Moon ○	13
14	15	16	17	18	19 Last Quarter ◐	20
21	22	23	24	25	26	27 New Moon ●
28	29	30	31			

September

Sunday	Monday	Tuesday	Wednesday	Thursday	Friday	Saturday
				1	2	3 First Quarter ◑
4	5 Labor Day	6	7	8	9	10 Full Harvest Moon ○
11	12	13	14	15	16	17 Last Quarter ◐
18	19	20	21	22 Autumn Equinox	23	24
25 New Moon ●	26	27	28	29	30	

October

Sunday	Monday	Tuesday	Wednesday	Thursday	Friday	Saturday
						1
2	3 First Quarter ◑	4	5	6	7	8
9 Full Hunters Moon ○	10 Indigenous People's Day	11	12	13	14	15
16	17 Last Quarter ◑	18	19	20	21	22
23 / 30	24 / 31 Halloween	25 New Moon ●	26	27	28	29

November

Sunday	Monday	Tuesday	Wednesday	Thursday	Friday	Saturday
		1 First Quarter ◐	2	3	4	5
6	7	8 Election Day Full Beaver Moon ○ **Eclipse**	9	10	11 Veterans Day	12
13	14	15	16 Last Quarter ◐	17	18	19
20	21	22	23 New Moon ●	24 Thanksgiving Day	25	26
27	28	29	30 First Quarter ◐			

December

Sunday	Monday	Tuesday	Wednesday	Thursday	Friday	Saturday
				1	2	3
4	5	6	7	8 Full Cold Moon ○	9	10
11	12	13	14	15	16 Last Quarter ◑	17
18	19	20	21	22	23 New Moon ●	24 Christmas Eve
25 Christmas Day	26	27	28	29	30 First Quarter ◐	31 New Year's Day

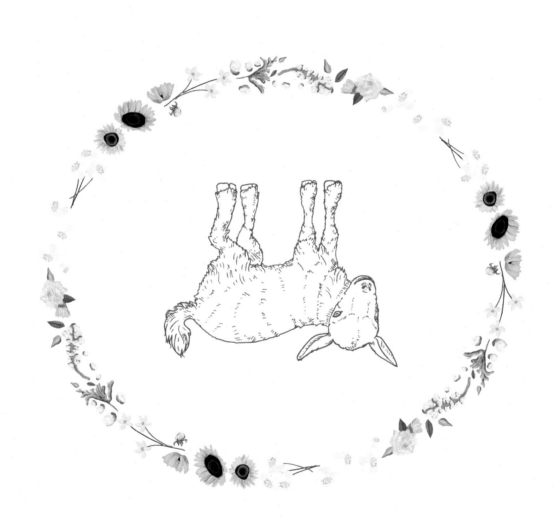

Made in the USA
Monee, IL
06 March 2022

92357487R00017